T0197204

JOURNAL

Me The Broken

BALBOA.PRESS
A DIVISION OF HAY HOUSE

Balboa Press books may be ordered through booksellers or by contacting:

Balboa Press
A Division of Hay House
1663 Liberty Drive
Bloomington, IN 47403
www.balboapress.com
1 (877) 407-4847

Print information available on the last page.

ISBN: 978-1-9822-4580-1 (sc)
ISBN: 978-1-9822-4581-8 (e)

Balboa Press rev. date: 04/06/2020

CONTENTS

ABOUT THE BOOK

My story isn't meant to be compared with other stories. My point is not an attempt to show you how bad I was or how broken I may have seemed to others, but rather harness how broken I felt inside so those who carry the same or similar storm within them can relate. I ask that when reading this you look for similarities rather than differences. If you are like me or understand anything shared, then you know some of the words I will use in this book will have a far greater depth to them than for those who don't suffer in silence. Words like dread, anger, resentment, loneliness, and maybe even hate have ripped through me often enough to eat away at my self-worth, and any lingering confidence until they cease to exist within me. Words like happiness, pride, and peace were things so elusive that I would question if they could even be meant for me. I began to believe that those positive emotions were designed for Hollywood, self-help teachings, and the kid next door. From the outside it should have looked like a comfortable middle-class life, but on the inside an emotional storm was beginning.

ACKNOWLEDGMENTS

- All the addicts and alcoholics in and out of recovery that has paved the road of misery with the importance of life.
- Adult Drug Treatment Court Program for providing the training-wheels of accountability and responsibility long enough for me to learn to ride.
- My once therapist and now a friend. You have shown me it is not always about the money
- My wife, for showing me that no matter how much or how great our losses are we can still be happy. Also for supporting me no matter what.
- Family and friends who stood by me on my journey
- My attorney and great support
- My grandmother, for being the mother I never had, and the one I always needed
- Recovery sponsors, for handing me the missing keys to make this life possible

I dedicate this book to my father who fought to the end and opened a door to my truth, my grandfather, for never giving up on me, and God because none of this happens without him! I know they are all together pulling for me today. Until we are together again, I love you.

God bless!

JOURNAL

My enemy was born in October of nineteen seventy-five to an alcoholic dad and a mom who wasn't very emotionally stable either. Within a couple years I was left by my mom to be raised by my grandparents. Although my grandparents did a wonderful job raising me like I was their own child, knowing my mom had abandoned me and watching my dad chose beer over me was harder to take every day. Unfortunately, my family values had become distorted, and I was too ashamed to talk about this happening to me. Coming up as a product of a broken family forced me to compare my life with other families. This starting me out scorekeeping right away and I always seemed to lose. A good thing about having my grandparents as backup parents is that it freed my dad up from participating in my life, and saved me the embarrassment of having to be seen with him. My dad fit the social stigma of an alcoholic, or at least I felt he did. He had dark hair, often greasy, scraggily, and his clothes were often dirty. Most people either didn't notice or didn't care but I sure did. He looked nothing like the other dads, and my lack of knowledge of alcoholism left me with nothing to defend myself with. It seems kind of silly looking back on my dad now, I don't recall ever needing to defend him or myself.

In kindergarten I felt so uncomfortable playing with the other kids that I would stay on the other side of the classroom. I remember one day a bully came over to take part of the wooden train I was playing with and took the engine and then he proceeded to pick on me. The anxiety ripped through me causing enough anger that I smacked him in the face with a different part of the train. The teacher separated us and said she would call my dad to come get me. I was horrified, I thought, "How can this get any worse" and I sat waiting for the embarrassment to come and show himself to the other kids. They would be sure to pick on me even more when I go back tomorrow, I thought. When my grandpa showed up, I of felt such relief for,a couple reasons. First of all I wouldn't be embarrassed by my dad, and second when the teacher told the story of what happen my grandpa was angrier with her than me. Unfortunately this was a short lived victory, and the next one would be far away. I played by myself during recess a lot of the time. When I didn't I was of always filled with anxiety and nervousness.

I did catch a couple breaks in life. The few friends I had all lived within a couple miles from me in either direction. Two friends, Mark and Joe were neighbors for about eleven years so I was able to trust them enough to feel somewhat comfortable around them. I had three other friends, Sean, Frank, and Steve, who lived close by, so on occasion we all played football or rode dirt bikes together. That was the extent of it until I was around thirteen years old.

Let's go back to about the age of seven. I started going to church with a friend of mine. My Grandparents had told me it would be good for me to go to church and besides I figured people would have to be friendly.

I was wrong, dead wrong. I found I couldn't see clearly through the anxiety and I was sure I didn't belong. Later I got separated from Steve before a prayer session. I was just riddled with fear when they put me in a room full of kids I didn't know. Social anxiety coursed through me like being burned from the inside. While the adults attended regular service I was placed in a small classroom with a bunch of strangers and I became emotionally and mentally bankrupt almost instantly. The teacher asked us to pray to be "saved" by Jesus, and I thought, "I am in a church, and about to be saved by Jesus himself. I thought, "Cool this will make me feel at least little better, maybe normal even!" So we prayed, and then individually we got called on to ask if we prayed, and how we felt as a result. As soon as my name was called, and I had to speak in front of those other kids, I felt that sheer hell of anxiety flow through me like never before. I lied because I didn't want the others to know Jesus didn't love me. It was that moment, I began to believe that Jesus don't want me, or at the very least was too busy for me. I replayed all the miracles that I had heard Jesus had done and couldn't see how I would possibly be harder to help than them. I became angry and bitter towards the church, the pastor, and that damn religion, even to Steve and his family. I remember riding home with my friend and his parents and thinking, "What is so wrong with me?" "What is special about them?" "Why in the hell did you even create me if you want nothing to do with me?" These thoughts began to shed light on the idea that maybe I am here as a, "What not to be" kind of person the pastor talked about.

I believe today that it was that moment when I began to question not the existence of God, but rather the existence of God in my life. I begged my grandparents to prevent me from going to church again. When others talked about how they couldn't see how going to church all the time did any good I jumped on that train like I was headed to Disney World. I joined anyone who stood up against having to go to church. I felt guilty when I had to face Steve after he asked me if I would be going to church with them. I would make up excuses as to why I couldn't go. No one else in our group was on board with the church idea so I felt bad turning my back on him. I often felt like he was happy to finally have a friend go along. Unfortunately if God didn't want me to go to church, then he should go with Steve instead is what I told myself. I really started to put some serious thought into my identity and purpose. Being a lost cause began to make more sense as I turned the idea over in my mind. I started to believe that maybe this is why my dad drank so much, and maybe even why my mom left. It made me draw pity on my grandparents. After all they got stuck with me I figured.

Going to school was horrible at times, because anxiety made me feel like a social outcast. I was always plagued by the "What ifs?" What if I wasn't cool enough, smart enough, funny enough, and so on. Those what-ifs held me as prisoner of loneliness, and fear was the warden. Loneliness was overwhelming at times, no matter what size of a group I was in, if any. All too often I would stay up to late on school nights and then be impossible to wake up in the morning. I would run behind so I wouldn't comb my hair good, eat breakfast, among other things. Not doing these little things would only compound the feelings of not belonging and loneliness. Fear that I would be picked on consumed me to the point that even if I want to talk or join something I couldn't allow myself to be exposed for my lack of self-care. My grandparents spoiled me to make up for the lack of parenting I received. Lack of discipline and direction only helped to fuel my social issues. I feel fortunate to be smart enough to understand this, but I lacked the discipline needed to fix it. I sure couldn't bring myself to say anything. In the fourth grade I found enough courage to change my hairstyle and I was ridiculed for it by more than half of the class. I remember my mind ran through every scenario it could so I could escape. Thoughts of what I would do to them all if I ever became "someone" played over and over. The worst part about being bullied for something is that it doesn't stop after you correct it. Nope, they keep drilling just to break you over and over at the expense of your happiness just to satisfy theirs. My resentment machine played to the point it forced me to imagine that inside of me was a superhero waiting to emerge. I realize now that if my mind would not of done this I may have found another outlet for my aggression, and God only know what that may have been. I made up and pretended that I was a better hero than Spiderman, or Superman. I lived it in my head for the remainder of my elementary school career.

About a year later I found a lock box in my dad's room and it was unlocked. I realized I had never seen it before and wondered where it came from. I took a look inside and found letters from my mom. I was excited, and hurt all at the same time. I began to read the letters. I found one from my dad's girlfriend that said "He better not be with that bitch!" I assumed this meant my mom. I found myself upset at this and decided when I was bigger I would have a chat with her about calling my mom names. After reading a few, I ran across a letter that would change my life and give me a whole new outlook on family. The letter said to my dad that they had made a mistake. After a few more lines, the words jumped off the page and slapped me. She said, "I didn't want him, only you!" My heart broke, for that was the proof of all proof. It summed up why my dad drank, why Jesus didn't save me, why my mom left, and maybe worst of all, why my poor grandparents got stuck raising this throw-away. I spent the next four years trying to suppress the thoughts. I kept telling myself she was missing out not me, among other things. I finally settled on hate, it was easier to come by and resentment took very little effort to maintain, or so I thought. The problem with resentment is that I grew comfortable enough with it. I could believe the lie when I told others "I don't care about her!" However that wasn't true and when it was added to the rest of the pain and negativity going on my sub-conscious was screaming for relief. Don't get me wrong, the good times playing football, and hanging out with friends did help. Unfortunately I was a time bomb, and my sickness was feeding on it. I began to look for things to set me apart from the others so I could build an identity that I could be proud of. It seemed like my friends were always "one-uping" each other and I was desperate to have the sun shine on me one day. I was sure that when that moment would finally arrive I would be free of the bondage of self that I was cursed with. I knew the few times I could muster up the courage to push the limits fear of being able to continue the success set in so I decided not to over brag the situation or achievement too much.

It occurred to me one day that maybe pushing the physical limits wasn't for me. I decided to try more adult-like options. I believe this idea popped into my head after realizing I felt more comfortable while talking with some of the parents more than the friends. Over time the need to grow up became more enticing. I began taking cigarette butts from the ashtray and smoking them. Enjoying the thrill I would get just from doing that demanded more. Over a short period of time the new wore off and the excitement started to fade. The idea popped in my head one day to see what my dad found great about drinking. After all I felt as though he replaced me with it. So here I sit in my room at approximately age eleven or twelve, when the thought crossed my mind, "What is it about this alcohol that keeps my dad a slave to it?" With that thought in mind I decided to give it my own evaluation. I went headed for my dad's room because I knew he wasn't around, and if anyone asked what I was doing I would just say I was looking for him. I reached his room, and looked at the beer and vodka supply. I decided that three Milwaukee's Best and some vodka would be a good test, plus they were warm and I didn't believe he would notice that little bit missing anyway. I headed back to my room, enjoying the excitement building inside of me. The thrill I got from just taking the alcohol should have been a red flag but at that age I figured who cares, it's only a one-time thing.

When I finally reached my room and sat down, my thoughts were all over the place. I remember smelling the vodka like a professional taste tester or critic. Swirling it around in an old plastic cup, I prepared myself to take a sip. As I slowly tipped the cup back and it hit my tongue, I remember jerking the cup away and cringing as if I ate an orange after brushing my teeth. It was horrible tasting so I set the cup down and thought maybe the beer would be better.

I cracked open the warm can, and I also cracked open hell, although I didn't know it yet. I smelled the beer, and although I wasn't real impressed, it did seem as though it would not burn or be as harsh as the vodka going down. I took a smaller sip than before with the vodka. Between the reliefs of it not tasting as bad, and the excitement still running through me I drank the beer down. I opened the second beer and started on it, but this time I added sips of the vodka. By the time I had finished the third beer and the vodka I had some understanding of my dad's desire for it. The release from self was wonderful. I had never felt such freedom, peace of mind and such fearlessness. It was as if I finally entered the world I had been denied so long. I felt how I viewed others around me. The feeling that I had finally arrived was profound. Although I'm sure this didn't make me alcoholic, it should have been a sign that the thoughts of doing it again was exciting. Being able to look through the eyes of those I viewed as well-established socially, was a dream come true.

I took advantage of the opportunities to feel out how others thoughts about drinking. I know now that it was my attempt to put "feelers out" for future recruits. It was nice not being alone while trying not to be alone. I did this a few times, even offered a beer or two to those willing.

One day my aunt told me she had met a new friend that had a son. I met a new friend named Chuck when I was almost twelve. He was a couple years older than me and he was outside my small group of current friends. This was nice for me because I felt like I had something the others didn't, and I enjoyed the new victory on life. We were extremely close for about two years until he moved out of state. I went to visit him the next two summers but the last summer I went it got cut short due to driver's training. As life went on I began to realize that time was making a stranger out of my once best-friend. I would often ask, "God why do you keep taking them all away from me?" Although I am sure the answer was there I just failed to see it and the thoughts of being a mistake would consume me hard and longer every time.

Entering high school was extremely difficult because the anxiety was very hard on me. It opened up the social flood gates and allowed my isolated little world to be infiltrated by new people. This anxiety brought about the memories of the few isolated drinking episodes I had. This also would mean that while circles of people grew the possibility of more people meeting my dad grew with it. At this point I had already helped my dad off the bathroom floor a couple times because he freaked out while hallucinating during an attempt to detox. No matter how bad I wanted to hate him I found I couldn't help but feel my heart break watching a full grown mad curled up screaming, "Get 'em off me!" while on the cold tile floor scratching at his arms. High school did have one immediate perk; the drive to be so secretive about drinking began to vanish. I could put feelers out again but now I could be more open because all tough guys in school talked about partying. Strangely enough I met a girl named Tori who was willing to take turns on occasion putting a fifth of vodka in our lockers to mix with our pop. Although it didn't happen a lot it did bring some relief in knowing I wasn't alone, especially since she was a more popular student, who carried a more "I don't give shit!" attitude. I fell in love with the emotional freedom she introduced me to, and felt I was placed on a new social level because of her good looks and popularity. The few times I went to her house I seemed to get along with her parents. This was nice because I got the feeling they didn't trust anyone she hung out with, and probably for good reason. I was scared of her social status and locked myself in to a "friend-zone" position that later became a bigger problem for me. I was so proud to be hanging around her that I soon introduced her to my small group of friends and she soon hooked up with my new best-friend Tom. This was a crushing blow in my attempt to escape me. Although I didn't entirely lose her, I began to get in to more trouble in school just to get suspended. When you got suspended at my school they would send you to another building off campus and I would be placed in a cubical to do my school work. Although I am sure this appeared to be a great idea to the educators, it placed me in eight hours of silence with my demons. I would get suspended often because it saved me from the social awkwardness I felt at school. I know longer had to lie, to act, to pretend while I sat in isolation, and besides I could almost call it home. Don't get me wrong here, I don't wish to over sell my misery. In fact I had tons of great times and happy days.

As we partied I slowly became a little better at getting out as long as I could drink or keep the circle of people small. It was hard to use fads to fit in because my grandparents wouldn't buy the expensive clothes and shoes. My rate of maturity was stunted by the drinking and the fear of change more and more. As I made attempts to reach outside my circle to replace "Chuck" I traded a rifle I got from my dad that didn't work for a handgun. I didn't like the handgun after a short time so I traded the handgun for a shotgun that had some very cool wood burning art done to the stock. I just wasn't very big in to hunting so the gun became a dust collector in the back of a closet.

One day in tenth grade I was pulled out of class and told that I would be placed in a ninth grade English class because I was lacking in required credits. I was terrified. I couldn't help but wonder how dumb I had to look to everyone. I sat in the back of that class, quiet, in hopes to just slide by undetected. Then one day a girl called from another town that I had kind of dated a few times and told me she was having a party. I rallied the troops but only got about eleven people to go. Once we all passed out, we were woken up by about 30 people who apparently were not too happy. Although the details are sketchy a fight broke out and we didn't fair too well. I escaped and made it to my car but knew I couldn't leave until all of my friends were safe. So I popped the trunk and removed the longest screw driver I could find and ran back to battle. Although I don't remember first-hand account of what happened, but I struggled and fought off a few guys as an attempt to elude any further beating I was getting. Suddenly Tom comes out of nowhere hits a guy holding me, and I only remember breaking free and making a dash to my car. By this time most of us were finding our vehicles and getting out while we could. I know a friend of mine Mark was with me and he had real long hair. I over-heard someone yell "Find that long haired guy, because he just f#cking stabbed me!"

Then Monday back at school I was catching strange looks and watching whispers as I passed by small groups talking. When I arrived in that ninth-grade English class it only got worse. My anxiety was through the roof. I was close to just snapping on someone when finally the kid in front of me turned and said, "Did you stab a guy?" I told him it wasn't me, but he just winked and said, "Ok, got ya!" It didn't take me long to realize I could cash in on this socially. Truth is, the moments before that guy claims he got stabbed are a blank to me. Something told me to get my friend Mark out of there so he didn't pay for my actions. The mind is a powerful thing. It almost has its own agenda and ways of dealing with things at times of stress and tragedy.

I did my best to capitalize on my new reputation. In the eleventh grade I was finding I had more of a backbone, and my friend count was growing. The problem I was facing is that I knew I was truly a coward who was riding on the coattails of a past situation that had manifested out of pure fear and hiding behind friends I didn't think I could even compare with. At least this is what my mind would constantly tell me. Socially my dad had become more popular than I did in ways. I'm sure a good portion of that was due to the fact he was our ticket to beer. We had cars and a license but needed beer, and he didn't have a car or license but need beer also. Most everyone liked my dad, and why not, he had a great personality. He laughed and joked around plus he was one of guys, just not one of mine. I watched the alcohol slowly consume him in many ways. I watched as his appetite diminishing slowly and the alcohol increased. In just a few years a small framed pale skin man had become bloated and yellow from jaundice. His friendly fun loving personality dwindled down as the self-pity and fear consumed him. I remember watching my dad cling to a Bible which I found odd at first. Over time I began to realize my dad knew he was running low on time and this sparked a need for God in his life. My dad had continued going to church even after I graduated high school.

By the end of the eleventh grade I had met a beautiful blond that just fixed everything in me instantly. Carry and I were together about four years and I was a King finally. It was if all my struggles had finally paid off. I watched guys look with jealous eyes and envy all over their faces. I was setup with a good job through the aid of my school shop teacher. I even was given the chance to stay enrolled in school and not actually have to attend for one more year. I did this so I could walk in graduation with Carry, to show off that I had finally arrived. You see I was somehow a half credit short on my needed credits. All I need was an extra-curricular class credit so I signed up on a work experience program using the job my shop teacher got me. When I first got the news about my credit, I was ready to throw in the towel. I wanted out of that social prison so bad, a half credit was enough to so say hell with it all. Had Carry not ask me to walk with her on graduation, and my shop teacher make it possible for me to not have to go back to receive my credit, my diploma may have ceased to exist today. I have no doubt this would have drastically changed the course of my recovery efforts and security today. I had to show the world that I have arrived! You see the outside beauty of Carry trumped all the inside ugliness that either one of us had. I became so blind that in the beginning I damn near worshiped her. Over time my brokenness began to show up in narcissistic behavior. I would push her limits until we reached a breaking point and then pleaded for her to forgive me over the fear of losing her. The real bad part of this is that wasn't even true; I knew I'd be like a chameleon unable to change color. I could no longer hide me, leaving me vulnerable to the world again. My broken side was even broken. I couldn't differentiate the true from the false. It wasn't losing her that scared me the most; it was seeing me for who I really was. I had used her and didn't know I was doing it. She was my identity, my social glue, because deep down I was sure if she left I would be nothing again. Being a slave to her had forced me to rebel and become narcissistic, the need to be my own person was screaming to come out and I failed to understand it. Of course that really didn't matter because I would have failed building my own person anyway.

After four years of what I seen as a perfect relationship she left one day. I came home from work blind-sided by an empty place and loneliness. I absolutely went crazy, the ability to control myself in any form seemed impossible. I pulled the stalker style behavior and humiliated myself more every day. I drank to the point I couldn't make it to work. My job was slipping away and my life was an absolute mess. I let people move in and party because it kept the thoughts of suicide at bay. I was hiding money from myself and forgetting where I put it because I was so drunk the night before. I did whatever I could to drown the memory of the greatest thing that ever happened to me. I took full blame for her leaving because self-pity was my new best friend.

About a month after she had left me, my dad passed away from alcoholism. He had moved out of state because of the shame he caused himself. My dad had burned down the family home at one point after he had passed out drunk. Losing my dad and my girlfriend within a month and a half was very hard on me. Not realizing it then, but that started to accelerate my drinking even more. I joined a traveling billiard pool league to occupy my time. This introduced me to methamphetamine for the first time. I would shoot pool at night, drink, and then go right to work. Finally after a few weeks of doing this I lost my temper at work. All the bottled emotion came pouring out. I was finally let get go from that job for a number of things really.

I finally gave up the place and moved back home because the responsibilities were too much for me to deal with both mentally and emotionally. I remember after moving home I would have long talks with my grandfather at early morning hours about the pain of heartbreak. One night he woke up to go to the bathroom and caught me standing by the door and asked where I was going. He didn't know it then, but I had talked myself into suicide for the most part. I was pushing for that last ounce of motivation when he stopped me. My grandpa was my rock, and my hero. One of the most selfless men I have ever met. Every so often the thought popped in my head that I didn't deserve him, but I sure did need him.

I attempted to move a few times in hopes the new start would bring about sufficient change for my life. I moved in with Mark and Joe's dad on the lake by my grandparents. They were my neighbors growing up but sold that house to Tom's dad, and they moved to a house on the lake. That was great for a long time, but the unemployment ran out and I had no job. Tom had since moved and started a business about two hours away. I contacted him in hopes to gain employment and to outrun my demons. Tom and his brother were some of the greatest eye-openers I could have asked for. I was finally motivated to grow, and to be myself. Unfortunately I grew homesick after a year I returned home for the winter and decided to stay.

The best part about it was I had finally received driving privileges back from an impaired driving I received over a year earlier. I was a new man, and eager to prove it. The first thing I did was run back to the old hang-outs to say, "Hi," and that was all it took. I was back to my old broken self again.

I went to jail one night on a drunk-driving charge. The next morning I called the bar owner where I was at the night before to ask for a ride home. Once I got home, I knew I was in bad shape. I went and picked my truck up, and stayed away from the bars for a while because they were getting me in trouble I thought. I was out at my friend Mark's house one day when I received a call to sub on a pool league at a local bar. I was quite reluctant at first but that old voice in the back of my mind spoke right up and said go. When I got the bar I was given a drink ticket for one free drink and I used it. As we were all shooting pool it was brought to my attention that almost no one else drank. I ended up with about twenty-three free drink tickets total. I drank everything from beer, shots and mixed drinks.

When the league ended I couldn't even walk. I had fallen over a table and a chair just trying to leave the bar. In a moment of clarity I had given my keys to a designated driver. Unfortunately he couldn't drive a standard transmission. After what I felt was good justification I started my truck and drove away. About a third of the way home I caught myself nodding out and unable to focus. I realized that I was on a straight shot to my friend Mark's house. I rolled the window down in my truck, put Alanis Morrisette in the CD player, lit a smoke, and headed towards my one mile destination.

I woke up in the hospital, scared, confused and throwing punches. A doctor walked in and asked me a series of questions; one of them being, "Do I know why I am there?" I told him I didn't but it was obvious something had happened to me because my lower jaw was kicked to one side. He explained to me that I had been involved in a car train collision and that I was lucky to be alive. Apparently my response was not good because he became agitated and explained to me the differences in percentages of fatality rates in various types of train accidents. All of which I thought were high, and he assured me they were not. In that moment I felt guilt, shame, embarrassment, among other things. I didn't need a mirror or anyone else there to know that I am becoming my dad, the man I thought I hated. I was a major let down to my grandparents since my dad passed from drinking, and my uncle was well on his way. Windows of reality just kept popping up until all I wanted to do was crawl off in to a hole and never be found. I was angry with myself, God, and the guy who couldn't drive a standard transmission. I cursed in that hospital bed and asked God, "Why do you not take me?" I thought to myself, "I don't need more proof of being a mistake. I already had enough!" It was obvious no matter how good I tried to be, my life was cursed.

After weeks of blending food and facing people with my shame I finally got the wire system removed from my mouth. I stopped by a friend's place and he asked me if I was going to keep drinking. I told him no, and he told me how he quit. Having used cocaine and meth in the past it wasn't exactly a new thing, but I never realized I could use it against my drinking problem. As I began to realize that meth had helped me escape my desire to drink other thoughts popped in to my mind. Thoughts like, now I won't fall asleep driving, cops wont smell beer on my breath, and I can pass a breathalyzer if I get pulled over. This meth idea was starting to become a real win I thought.

Eventually I was placed on house arrest for my drinking and driving with nothing left to do but play on the computer, and wait for my dealer to stop by. I began to mess around in multiplayer based games. It was kind of strange to realize that my social anxiety was almost as bad on the internet as it was in person. Over time I found some regular friends on some games that I could talk with. I remember once a girl asked me to leave the game and chat in private. That same fear I have had with ladies in real life was just as glaring to me in a private internet chat. I lied to escape the situation and quickly logged off the computer.

When I was finally off of house arrest I avoided the bars but began to hang out with those who understood my drug use. The narcotics never really relieved me from my social anxiety. At some point I actually started to miss my internet friends because I didn't have to hide so much. I finally realized the best thing to do was to get my dope, and go play on the computer. I taught myself web-coding, graphic design, and gaming. I started building computers and fixing them on trade for drugs and money. I was having trouble supporting my habit and full time jobs got in the way of my using. I began to pay close attention to the talk amongst drug makers and dealers. I figured out a lot oftranslation of.

- Back to Basics: Faith Without Works publishing has a greatly simplified break-down for helping people understand how the twelve-step programs work.
- Me The Broken on Facebook, or look me up at Methebroken.com

I got a couple of Sponsors from AA (Alcoholics Anonymous) because it is too easy to misread, misinterpret, or just simply overthink this stuff. Most people can do the work in a matter of hours or days. If you don't have a substance problem then, by all means, seek professional or religious help for guidance. Accountability and proper understanding of our thinking are critical, only another person can see us for who we truly are.

RIGHT AND WRONG

I had not planned on a right and wrong topic, but since I brought it up I guess I had better clarify what I meant. Throughout my life, if something didn't line up with my understanding then I would assume it to be wrong unless I was able to see how it could better me and then it was right. The problem is with right and wrong is every time I used them in my head It would open or close my mind on a given subject or situation. This can rob a person of growth later, and it drastically impacts humility. So I have learned to adopt a way of thinking that replaces the words "right and wrong" with "better or worse" when it comes to growth. If you ever read a part of the Bible or some self-help book today and then go back sometime later and reread that same part, you may find it no longer applies the same in your life. This does not make what you read wrong, it simply means you have changed and as a result, the words impact you differently. Hold on to this thought because we will need it later also. You see when a person reads something or hears something that betters their life it should be viewed as a better way, not the right way. This helps to keep the mind from shutting the door on the possibility that it may change or find a better way later. The same way with wrong and worse, if we do something and it does not make it better than we should remember it made it worse not wrong. I can come up with a lot of reasons and examples of this way of thinking. For instance, if I am not as far along in my life as you and you tell me that this is the right way to do a job or task and it doesn't work, then a number of things can happen. Sometimes advice won't work out and I may view the information as wrong, when in fact the frame of mind I am in just does not allow me to see it at that time. If I shut the door on the advice I may never go back and review it later when I could actually apply it. If I take the advice and I deem it right and not better, then I may never push for growth in that area again. So when helping or giving advice try to keep right and wrong out as much as possible. This is also why self-awareness is so important because when we do help someone out we can be more accurate on why something did or didn't work well. I'm sure some of you are thinking, "I already understand this," well good, but if we don't apply what we understand then it only becomes a dust collector in the mind. This might seem like a small thing at first but let me assure you, all of the things in this book can be viewed as small to one person or another, but it's the little things that get us in the end. In addition, by adding all of the little things together, you have one fulfilling life.

FEELINGS

I want to clarify my perspective on feelings as a whole. Feelings are not facts! Feelings, for the most part, can be traced to the thoughts, which can be traced to my beliefs. So if my beliefs are wrong, then my thoughts may be wrong, now my feelings may be wrong. Sometimes my lack of confidence would have me on high alert when a girl talked to me. I would be hunting for signs that she may like me enough to go farther than our current conversation. This drive would trigger desire and excitement allowing me to think I see signs that were not actually present. I would feel so good about it that I may place myself in a position to be rejected or let down. For someone like me, this feeling can be very hard to take, humiliation can be devastating to a person, especially someone who unknowingly is pursuing something or someone to fill an emotional void or spiritual hole. Here is another scenario; what if a person appears to be staring at me or checking me out? My mind will usually tell me "I must have done something wrong!" So this belief will trigger a thought that in turn will drum up a negative feeling. Truth is in either of the above cases I need to get the facts that will properly direct my feelings, and not allow my feelings to dictate as facts. Once I am proven wrong by leading with feelings I have found that my next go-to is justification which has a tendency to drag out a situation longer than it needs to and also makes it worse. The only person that ever really cares that much or buys it anyway most of the time is the person selling it. Even those that attempt to co-sign my feelings as facts don't usually feel I am right, they just try to make me feel better. Does this mean that feelings can't be trusted? Feelings are used more as indicators, but they really should not be trusted until our thought and belief system can be. If I don't fix that belief system I will find myself, restless, irritable, and discontented leaving me most often bitter, angry and resentful. This can lead to seeking out quick fixes for relief such as drinking, drugs, sex, and gambling, among other things. Today I see how anger played an active role in my life on a daily basis. Anger is a thief of happiness, and not just ours, it is a justifier of bad behavior and beliefs. Anger robs us of precious time that could be spent enjoying our life. I have said in the past that I wish I had one more day with someone who has passed away. After I began to look at all the ridiculous stuff that I became angry about for days or weeks over at a time I soon realized that I had my day(s), but I wasted them on anger. Sometimes I wasted those days in anger against the very person I wish I had one more day with. Anger can cover up other feelings to protect our pride and egos also. It is important to understand our feelings and get them right-sized. So the best way to fix our feelings is to fix our false beliefs and misunderstandings. I don't believe this is a complex task by any means. Willingness and time are all that is required, and ultimately both are up to you, at least those are my findings.

JUSTIFICATION

Here is what I found to be a very sneaky yet powerful force of negativity. It stems from so many things and shows itself in many forms. So I will do my best to cover this and give you at least a good skeleton idea solid enough for you to bring about your own awareness. If I could actually harness hate and have it not hurt me, justification in negativity or to put-off I believe is where I would aim it. Justification in positive growth should almost be self-explanatory. The size of justification is huge so I am going to start by giving out some examples of negative justification to avoid. Do not justify anything when struggling. Thoughts or statements that start out with, "What if, yeah but, I think that," among others need to be avoided in times of struggle. If you find yourself hurting or lost during any emotional, mental, or spiritual hardship ask for help. Do not satisfy an answer in your mind until proven trustworthy. Earlier I spoke about being stuck in the mud and spinning your wheels, well that applies here in many ways. Every time we justify an answer and it fails we lose the drive to actually find the real answer. Over time we end up saying things like "who cares," or "no big deal," and what we are really doing is saying "I refuse to grow," and that I am letting myself settle on a false belief. This gets easier over time to do, and we also pass it on to our friends, family, and even worse the raising of our children. In the end, I am afraid we will have raised a lost generation doing this. We can see this impact us even today. I have done it, and I have heard others do this ten times a day or more. If everyone does this can you imagine how many topics left unanswered, and how many false beliefs are left in place of the right ones, only to be passed on to others, who will, in turn, do the same until someone finally corrects it? Justification does this to important topics by making them appear small and harmless. After all, it is the little things that get us. So if you are uncertain, then admit it. Don't come to a false conclusion, leave it for review later. At the very least don't sell your uncertainty to others and allow ego to rob someone of finding the answers themselves. Because too someone else, this is a big deal!

EXPECTATIONS

Expectations are premeditated resentments. In fact, expectations in any form should cease to happen and I have yet an issue with doing this. Truth is the more I block expectations try to creep back in, the happier I am. About fifty percent of expectations are a form of negative justification. I grew up thinking that you should be able to expect certain things from people. Quite often I was let down even when they did happen because it still was not a satisfactory level. So here is a small list of expectations and ways to avoid them leaving you bitter.

- Anything you lend out is a gift. So if you can't afford to lose it then you must learn how to say no.
- Replace the word expect or expectation with the word Hope. Example: I hope my car starts when I leave here; not, I expect my car to start when I leave here. Believe it!
- Keep in mind all people are sick to some level and all the good that you feel you do does not necessarily prompt the same in return. (Integrity and humility are important here)
- Anything you wait for or look forward to can turn in to expectations (A good place to use hope).

So in any case, you find yourself stuck in expecting something, then simply follow it up with hope. Hence the saying, "Expect the worst, and hope for the best!" In waiting on someone or something I often replace it with hope, but when looking forward to something, I often say, "We'll see." At first, you may find people dislike hearing this but that is mostly due to the fact people place such high hopes on wants that they are not willing to accept anything less. Unfortunately, this is why expectations are so hard on people when they fail or don't satisfy a perceived outcome. A failed expectation also prompts us to fall into a negative justification of anger which only makes things worse. By losing expectations your worst case will be more tolerable, and your best case will be right-sized. Overall I have found a lot better balance in my emotional state especially in given situations that I had once carried favor one way or another. As far as those around me who have once disliked my right-sizing of expectations, most of them are on board with it now, and the ones who do not still seem happier. I can't live in fear of what others think anyway. This is my life and I deserve to maximize my true happiness.

FEAR

This subject was a huge problem for me when I started on my new path. The number of ways fears show up in a person's life was hard for me to believe at first. Here is a list of some of the more common ways fear has shown its face in my life. Most of the time I didn't even recognize it as fear, it just didn't register as the same thing.

- Anger
- Worry
- Anxiety
- Phobia
- Terror
- Panic
- Concern

This is by no means a comprehensive list but I believe it is sufficient to get us going. Fear works well with all character defects when it comes to breaking a person down. I have found fear can talk; it is that little voice that produces the "what-ifs?" I suffer from at times. For those on the spiritual journey already you can simply try and talk yourself into a reliance on God for the courage to face fears. If this is not an option I found it better to find what I am willing to face, then see if someone else has done it (most of the time yes). Understand that by the time I learned to face my fears and make the needed changes, I had worked the twelve steps and learned to utilize a simple reliance on God. Again having sponsors, spiritual advisors, or professional help can greatly increase courage and motivation by a simple means of support and encouragement. Selfish behavior and self-centeredness are driven by fear in so many different forms I can't even list them all here. It causes us to justify doing or not doing things that can help us or others and robs us of growth if we don't follow through. I have been faced with two types of fear in my life; healthy and unhealthy. Healthy fear most often does not need to be explained. Honestly most of the time I know to look before running into the road without looking, or jumping off a cliff. Quite often unhealthy fear will try and talk me into believing what I am facing is either no big deal or it's healthy to not do what I am facing. This is the critical moment I had to learn to push forward. I found it easier to start small and find a source of courage. I used the book, Alcoholics Anonymous, to establish my spiritual consciousness, which made it easier for me to find enough confidence to start facing my fears. Having a solid set of spiritual principals to live by is the key to start living, continue living, and grow while living. I'm not necessarily talking about any religious beliefs here. In fact, I found the spiritual principals can be used without any religious beliefs at all. I must learn to trust in a power greater than myself, rid myself of selfish behavior, and be of proper service to others. Spirituality was the component I had been missing when I went to church all those years ago, and its absence is what I lacked my whole life.

SPIRITUALITY

F irst of all let me start out by saying that there is no greater crime committed than a God lost to bad teachings, conversely there is no greater gift than a God found by any. This carries a lot of weight for people like me who started out in our own personal Hell. So when a person attempts to claw their way back to the real world they find themselves desperate to hold on to anything solid with even an ounce of hope that they are on their way. So, if I walk into a church and hold on to the beliefs I have been given through another's interpretation and I see them fail, I immediately slam the door shut against any ideal given. I rely on feeling and proof more as I become broken. A healthy person can often take the words of a trusted person and plant them with careful consideration. As an addict, I have found I automatically lack the ability to hold on to anything given without some level of contempt. So, when a person says "God loves you!" I may agree on the surface, and even want him to, but unfortunately, that lingering voice of doubt usually wins. The voice of doubt seems to win by persistence, not volume. This small voice I am referring to replaces that gut feeling and often leaves me with regret, usually leaving me thinking, "I knew it!" or, "I had a feeling that wasn't right!" Spirituality is the art of establishing trust in that gut feeling, a method of learning to rely on faith in that small voice of intuitive thought or decision. For me, religion, in the beginning, was a great concept and nothing more because I was missing the spiritual or divine connection it intended me to find. When you suffer from a spiritual sickness like addiction, the first thing attacked is the God-consciousness or connection with the Holy Spirit. This I believe happens through the genetics of kids born into addiction also. What Alcoholics Anonymous did was nothing more than establishing my Holy Spirit or connection with God. God will actually combat the malady for me provided I am willing to do the work. As a human, I am powerless over so many things and my ego would not let me believe it. In the beginning, I was first shown all the things I can do which in turn told me I was too smart ever fall victim to substance abuse. Once the idea that I won't ever be caught off guard is instilled, the malady begins to work on the rest of me. I think it is important to understand that addiction is not actually the problem; addiction is actually a failed solution to a problem. This failed solution binds us to a life of a living Hell, compounding bad choices on top of bad choices by not allowing us to differentiate the true from the false and we can't see the changes happening to us. This is why people are so powerless over addiction and why the medical community can't help us is because it is a spiritual sickness in which starts by choice and ends in slavery. This is also proof as to why some people can go so long without using any substance. No matter how long we go without using we are still bound by restlessness, irritability, and discontentment, and we can find no relief until we escape again. By not using, the malady understands that all we are doing is building up proof we are not sick, allowing us to one day return to using again in total confidence we don't have a problem. Two

God blockers are substance use and resentment, and the malady knows that by binding us to both so we are sure to lose. This is why justification and forgiveness are important topics to understand. I think alcoholics can be of higher intelligence in many cases and the malady knows this so it tells them they will be ok by reminding them of all they have done. Ego is a powerful tool of control. The same concept applies to an addict also; don't let them have time to think honestly and they will never be able to see his truth. The constant reminder of my past successes only brought about false hope that one day I will figure it out. Religion appears to allow a good portion of people a way to connect with God, and addiction is the disease that is a result of not having that needed link so spirituality is missed. Religion is for those who don't want to go to Hell, and spirituality is for those who don't want to go back. I found the best way to establish a spiritual connection is to simply admit your defeats, ask God for help, discuss your faults with another person to bring them out in the open, and start helping out your fellow person to stay outside of yourself. This is easier to do once we understand how forgiveness works. It also helps to get a handle on understanding faith, hope trust, and humility.

HUMILITY

Since we just talked about spirituality I would like to go right into humility. I believe humility is often overlooked in recovery. The only reason the twelve steps work is that it demands the humility to be its platform to start from. I think that this is why some people will say AA didn't work for them. AA doesn't work for anyone; it teaches you how to work for yourself. People think they can go sit in a meeting or do some reading and AA will somehow "poof" the problems away. I can see how entitlement issues stemming from selfish thinking allow them to believe that they are owed the solution to their troubles. I also believe that AA does not have a lock on recovery efforts but I still believe that the fault will always be on the person, not the program. This is true for many of those other recovery programs also. AA helped me by showing me how to look at myself and do an honest appraisal of my life. A lot of people, in general, are just not willing to entirely accept responsibility for their lives and may not wish to set right the wrongs they have caused because they feel justified in their actions. After all, if you try to steal my job by lying to the boss then I would feel compelled to get even or at least attack the person who is attacking me.

In the book Alcoholics Anonymous on page 62, it tells us that, "Selfishness—self-centeredness! That, we think is the root of our troubles. Driven by a hundred forms of fear, self-delusion, self-seeking, and self-pity, we step on the toes of our fellows and they retaliate. Sometimes they hurt us, seemingly without provocation, but we invariably find that at some time in the past we have made decisions based on self which later placed us in a position to be hurt. So our troubles, we think, are basically of our own making." So it stands to reason that if recovery requires humility to be the root of our efforts then it must be the direct combatant to selfishness. Below is not a comprehensive list in regards to humility vs. false humility but I hope will be enough to get us on the right track.

- *Real Humility should create a genuine concern for others, without any consideration for self-gain or credit. It is about putting others ahead of self*
- *Real Humility is about being of service to others through integrity. You should be able to escape any outside praise and feel rewarded only from within.*
- *Real Humility is about not only being able to admit your wrong but also apologize followed by changing your course to prevent it from occurring again. All three points are required, admit, apologize, and prevent. Of course, doing only one or two looks good but it does not build humility, and it takes a humble person to do so.*
- *Real Humility is required to grow with one's changes in responsibilities and power. If humility ceases to grow, things like ego, arrogance, and false pride begin to show.*
- *Real Humility will always build upwards, and false humility tears downward. False humility shows in taking credit and placing blame.*

Once humility becomes a working platform in my life I would have to assume the state of mind to follow would be humbleness. Humility does seem to work in levels as I grow so I found it important to keep working on it and watching for selfish behavior. Most people I talk to in recovery including myself, say how hard it is to recognize how far off track we have become because of how long we have been doing it. I found it was easy to grow comfortable in misery and bad habits. I justified them so long I could no longer see my wrongs or even the root of my troubles. I highly urge anyone willing to better themselves to at least first do an honest self-appraisal, or inventory of their character. This process is simple and can show you who you really are and where to start. I would encourage you to find a trusted person to be open with about yourself.

FAITH & TRUST

I misused the words wish, faith, hope, and trust so long I had never given them real thought. After catching myself using the word wish one time and hope later for the same situation it occurred to me that something is wrong. I began to look at the words and try to define them to see the differences. I have compiled the following for a process of my current understanding.

Wish > Faith > Hope > Trust

Wish   - *a conscious dream or want to consist of nothing more than thoughts or words. So if a wish comes true it builds faith.*

Faith - *having the belief that something is possible (trust in your heart)*

Hope - *the action was taken on said belief*

Trust   - *recognizing that the outcome has been or is being achieved.*

So if I make a wish and it comes true I build faith. Over time I rely on that faith as assurance. Next time I rely on that faith it brings hope due to the assurance I was given in the past. Once the outcome has been recognized I build trust.

To summarize:

When someone says they "hope" something happens, then one must assume they have "faith" otherwise it's just a "wish." When it happens I have either built "faith" or "trust." When I make a wish I am looking to build faith. When I say hope, I am looking to build trust.

FORGIVENESS

I really don't think a lot needs to be said about forgiveness. In fact, if humility is being achieved then I am somewhat sure most already understand it is important even if they don't understand why entirely. Forgiveness is often viewed or believed to be a sign of weakness or allowing. Forgiving someone or something is a means of power. Forgiving a person can be a very freeing action to take. The act does not condone the behavior or situation that wronged you it only means you are freeing yourself from its weight. Forgiveness allows a person to shed the negativity that you have been storing in your head and heart. Letting go can be a tough thing to do but the reward for doing so usually makes doing so well worth it. It does not always happen right away but over time you will have more energy, happiness, and peace of mind. I stated earlier that resentments are a God blocker, and this may be the largest reason for learning forgiveness. I have found the hardest things to do are usually the most important and provide the best impact on my growth. Amends are a form of forgiveness; it is also a way to let yourself off the hook for your past misdeeds. Even though you may not be the only bad part in a given situation if you stick to your own wrongdoing and attempt to repair the damage you will find it easier and easier to forgive yourself.

CONNECTED

Being connected through a sixth sense is the greatest ability I have been given to date. I am able to hear, feel and see on an entirely different level than I ever thought possible. I used to believe that this was a gift only given to select people; I now realize it is a gift meant for anyone, anywhere as long as the conditions are met. Before we get into the conditions let me first explain what we are talking about here. Prayer is simply talking to God, and meditation is simply listening to God. Unfortunately, I find this to be one of the most important aspects of my life and yet after talking to others it may be one of the most misunderstood, underused, and underappreciated gifts we have at our disposal. If I go into a gas station while lost on a family vacation to ask for directions, I would be sure to listen to the person helping me find my way. Yet when it comes to life we just keep driving around asking others who are lost and then not understanding why we can't find our way. This all too often leaves us blaming God for not helping us or at the very least keeping ourselves stuck in the mud spinning our wheels until we falsely satisfy our thinking with a bad belief or misunderstanding. This book and its topics are an idea of what areas I had allowed myself to remain broken for so long.

What I intend to do here now is bridge the gaps between God's will and self-will, plus spirituality and religion through God-consciousness, and two-way prayer. Religion can be a great belief structure if I can grasp spirituality, if I don't grasp the spiritual aspect then they stand a good chance of being disregarded as someone else's ideas and nothing more. Even if I do agree with the beliefs, all too often lack of spirituality will cause a person to lose importance or motivation in following them. It does appear however that some people can apply the beliefs found in the church and make a really blessed life in doing so, but others like myself seem to be missing a bridge or key component to making this work. This has left me feeling very uneasy, to say the least, and I became angry as stated in my story earlier. So let me get going on the conditions needed to fix and maintain a direct line of communication with the Great Creator.

I first had to surrender myself to the fact that I am powerless over a good portion of my life which includes but not limited to people, places, things like an addiction (yours or mine). I found it also necessary to do an honest self-evaluation or inventory. The book Alcoholics Anonymous has a wonderful set of simple instructions for doing this. Once I had discovered the truth about myself, both good and bad, I decided I had better come clean with someone I can trust. Now that I have offloaded the weight of my past and bad character it would be a great idea to help seal the deal with an amends plan. So any money I had owed I set up payments that I could afford and got right with those I had wronged, to the best of my ability. I should stress here that since this is an attempt to fix me as a person I should refrain from doing more harm in the process. So discussing others' faults or wrongs in a situation should be strictly prohibited. Only deal with your part in any situation. Don't expect (as I said earlier) to be forgiven by everyone, and don't expect anyone else to make amends to you on their part no matter how glaring it may be. Now that I have satisfied my past misdeeds or have at least started to, I can begin to work on those prayer conditions. This does NOT mean I should wait until now to pray, all I am suggesting here is this may be a good spot to work on that sixth sense I had talked about.

Let me get a few things straight here on prayer. God does NOT work for me, I work for him. Here are the conditions for establishing a two-way connection.

- *To relax your mind and thoughts so you can receive God's messages. Most literature tells us to be quiet and relax. I found I had to be able to achieve the state of mind needed to daydream. So I can go for walks or stand out on the deck to hear God, as long as the brain isn't active the body can be. I think this may apply to those minds that are more active. Over time I found that I got better at listening.*
- *Write down the thoughts that come during your time of meditation.*

We now have laws or rules to follow here. Once we receive thoughts from God it is important to follow instructions or directions given. God is willing to guide those who are willing to listen to him. This is not optional to pick and choose items. God is not an option or tool we use on bad days only. So when God speaks to you it is important to show him you hear him by doing what you are told. At first, this may seem absurd at times but I assure you that you are serving God to the best of your ability he will protect you and help you grow through any mistakes you make as a result. Over time you will get better and more confident in your conversations and following your instructions. To help get you started I will add a simple test below to help you be sure that the thoughts you have are God directed and are safe to listen to.

Here is why I asked you to write down your thoughts. Not every thought we have comes from God so to help ensure we don't get ourselves into trouble or off track we need to test all the thoughts that come into our head during our time with Him. This test can be applied throughout the day to our actions and attitude because you may receive more direction as you carry out your day. So to make sure I stay on track, anytime I have a decision to make, especially if it concerns someone else, I find it important to check the idea against the following standards to be sure what I am doing is healthy and does not carry hidden motives or negative influence. If any thought or action I have is resentful, selfish, dishonest, afraid, or fearful, then it is not healthy or God directed. However if what I am thinking is honest, pure, unselfish, and loving, then I can be satisfied I am on the right track. As I continue to do this it becomes a working part of my life. My energy levels increase because I am not spending it foolishly on negative living. I find that people seem to enjoy being around me and I tend to feel better overall, as well as having a heightened sense of awareness to situations.

Please keep in mind that we may not feel inspired at all times, and we also may find ourselves having intuitive thoughts that are hard to follow. Rest assured fear and doubt can happen, but the more you follow through and keep pushing, the greater the rewards and the easier it will get. God pays after we do the work quite often, so you should feel good about what you have done. This is a good indicator that you are on the right track. Keep pushing forward and you will soon see the changes that good God-conscious living will bring.

LOVE

I feel I would have drastically shorted this book and its purpose had I not talked about love. I need to end this book talking about the greatest gift ever given in both of its forms. Growing up I often associated love with relationships and the feelings. The human form of love is commitment. Earlier I spoke about how feelings are not facts, and now I will explain why this is true in love as well. I believe love is only given after a person follows through with an unspoken commitment. When growing up I heard people talk about how a relationship is work, and marriage is a commitment, and I often found myself uncertain if I really understood this. One of the bad beliefs I had was how love conquers all. Well, this is only half right. Love is a commitment can be extremely powerful, but as a feeling, it can be easily squashed if the commitment falls short. Love without commitment is just the new, and when the new wears off so does the drive to keep pushing. It is important to find gratitude for what I have even in the hardest of times. In doing so I find that my motivation and faith are soon restored and I can carry on usually better than before. When I talk about the commitment, I am talking about the commitment a person must make to themselves for themselves and not the hopeful promises that a person can't honestly keep.

When I feel lonely I use to think that if I had someone it would go away and all would be well. Truth is once I had someone I usually ended up losing sight of how lonely I felt and began to take the person for granted. Lonely is not a sign that I need someone, but it is an indicator that something is missing or wrong with me. No matter how sure I am no amount of external resources including people will ever actually fix my internal problems. I must learn to love myself without value placed on me by others. Once I can love myself completely, then and only then can I honestly give myself to another properly. Because I have satisfied my commitment, love as a gift can now be truly appreciated by me enough to honestly share with another person. I believe that until this happens the idea of a forever love is off the table. So if I am feeling lonely then I am bad company, and until I become a good company for me, I can't be a good company for anyone else. Just because I have achieved this understanding does not mean I am somehow able to coast or rest on this accomplishment. In fact, I have to keep honoring my commitment to myself which in turn allows me to honor this commitment with others. We can't let the feeling of love allow us to feel like we are somehow entitled to it. Love is the greatest feeling in the world when it is new. It is a divine "high" unmatched by any other. In the past, I would ride the feeling out for all its worth until it fades out of existence. Once it was gone I would curse it, and swear off on ever allowing it back in. I would complain about how bad it hurts and say that it isn't worth it. Love is not what hurts; it is the loss of love that hurts. Love does not change, we do! Yet I blame love for my mistakes. Love is more than a feeling, it is a commitment rewarded with a feeling. I found most often I stopped doing the work and expected others to continue to give it anyway. Love did not fail me, most of the time I failed it. I realize that most often two people are involved but truth is that it is still my fault because most of the time all the signs were there for me to see. My broken side was too afraid to admit it so I held on to what used to be with false hope. In short, it is important to listen to that small voice of reason. That voice saves me from being hurt by helping to guide me. I must choose to listen when I have feelings of doubt or uncertainty. That gut feeling, that small conscious reminder that something may not be quite right is the truth, an indicator in the dark. That voice is love, and it is spoken by God.

Printed in the United States
By Bookmasters